mel bay presents children's UKULELE method

by lee "drew" andrews

Cover instrument:
Kala Ukulele Acacia Soprano

CD contents

1	Tuning Track	18	Skip to My Lou	35	Ten Little Ukuleles	52	Jingle Bells
2	C chord	19	Jingle Bells	36	Down in the Valley	53	Up Strums
3	One beat rest	20	This Old Man	37	On Top of Old Smoky	54	Polly Wolly Doodle
4	Three Blind Mice	21	C note	38	E note	55	When the Saints Go Marching In
5	Half rests	22	Rest one	39	E - D	56	Careless Love
6	More half rests	23	Rest two	40	E - C	57	Corinne, Corinna
7	F chord	24	Whole note/D note	41	E - D - C	58	B note
8	Whole rests	25	Half note	42	Hot Cross Buns	59	B and A
9	Brother John (Frere Jacques)	26	Whole and Half note	43	F note	60	C note
10	Mixing chords #1	27	C and D whole notes	44	F - E - D	61	C, B, A
11	Mixing chords #2	28	C and D half notes	45	Halfsies	62	All the Notes
12	Row, Row, Row Your Boat	29	C and D quarter notes	46	Note Review (C - D - E - F)	63	The Bridge Melody
13	G7 chord	30	More quarter notes	47	G note	64	Happy Uke
14	Strumming C, F and G7	31	C note review	48	G - F - E	65	New 3/4 Strum Pattern
15	Pay Me My Money Down	32	D note review	49	A note	66	Home on the Range
16	London Bridge	33	It's Raining, It's Pouring	50	F - G - A exercises	67	My Bonnie
17	Three-Chord Progression	34	G chord	51	Twinkle, Twinkle Little Star	68	Oh, My Darling Clementine

LCCN: 2009941707

2 3 4 5 6 7 8 9 0

Visit us on the Web at www.melbay.com — E-mail us at email@melbay.com

table of contents

Parts of the Ukulele 3

Tuning 4

How to Hold the Ukulele 5

How to Strum the Ukulele 6

C Chord 7

Three Blind Mice 8

F Chord 9

Brother John (Frere Jacques) 10

What is a Measure? 11

Row, Row, Row Your Boat 11

G7 Chord 12

Pay Me My Money Down 13

London Bridge 13

Three-Chord Progression.........................14

Skip to My Lou 14

Jingle Bells 15

This Old Man 15

Playing Single Notes - C 16

Playing Single Notes - D 17

3/4 Time 19

It's Raining, It's Pouring 19

G Chord 20

D7 Chord 21

Ten Little Ukuleles 21

Down in the Valley 22

On Top of Old Smoky................................22

Playing Single Notes - E 23

Playing Single Notes - F 24

Playing Single Notes - G 25

Playing Single Notes - A 25

Twinkle, Twinkle Little Star 26

Jingle Bells 26

New Strum Pattern....................................27

Polly Wolly Doodle 28

When the Saints Go Marching In.................29

Careless Love 30

Corinne, Corinna 30

Playing Single Notes - B 31

Playing Single Notes - C 31

All the Notes...32

The Bridge Melody......................................32

Happy Uke 32

New 3/4 Strum Pattern................................33

Home on the Range....................................33

My Bonnie 34

Oh, My Darling Clementine 35

About the Author 36

I would like to thank the following: Elise Andrews, Bennie and Chris Andrews, Gary Davis, Mike Upton, Rick Carlson and my pals in the prep department at Mel Bay.

All interior photos, except page 3, by Gary W. Davis.

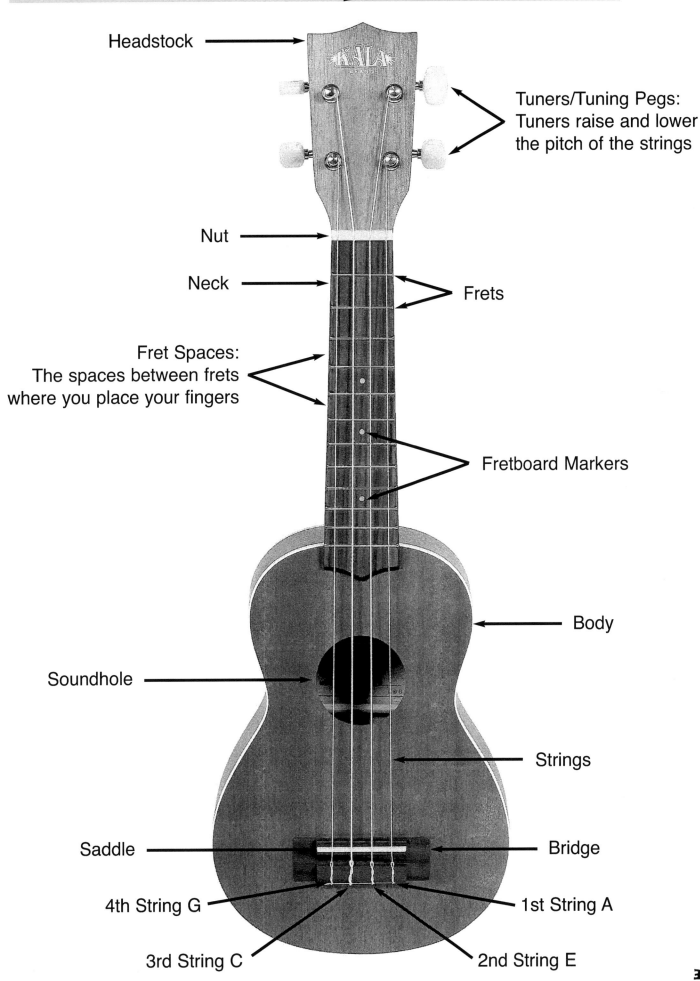

Headstock

Tuners/Tuning Pegs:
Tuners raise and lower
the pitch of the strings

Nut

Neck

Frets

Fret Spaces:
The spaces between frets
where you place your fingers

Fretboard Markers

Body

Soundhole

Strings

Saddle

Bridge

4th String G

1st String A

3rd String C

2nd String E

Tuning to a piano

The four open strings of the ukulele should be tuned to the match these notes on the piano.

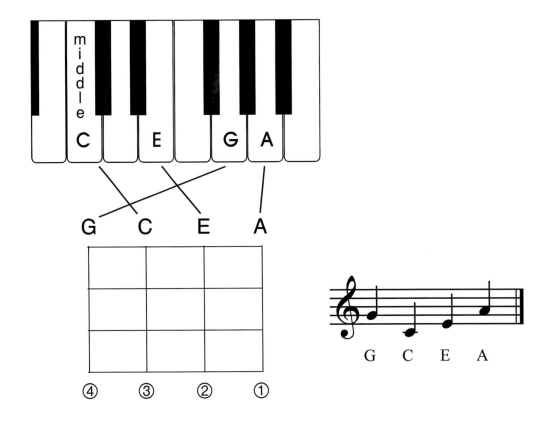

Although it seems odd, the G string is tuned higher than C or E. This is called a re-entrant tuning and is part of what gives the ukulele its unique sound.

 Track 1

Using an electronic tuner

Make sure you have a chromatic tuner.
1) If the tuner requires you to select a note choose G or which ever string you are tuning. If the tuner is automatic it will tell you the pitch of the string you are playing.
2) Lightly pluck the string.
3) Turn the tuner/tuning peg until the electronic tuner needle or indicator shows that the string is in tune. Repeat steps 2 and 3 for each string.

The CD that accompanies this book has a tuning track (Track #1) to help you tune your ukulele.

Match the pitches of your string to this track. Pitches are played in the following order: G, C, E, A.

how to hold the ukulele

Place the back of the ukulele against your body (upper stomach/lower chest). Hold it snug there with your right forearm. Make sure the neck of the ukulele has a slight upward angle. Your left hand will be on/somewhat support the neck of the instrument. Make sure your thumb is behind the neck. Tuck your left elbow in slightly.

Proper holding of the ukulele while standing.

Proper holding of the ukulele while sitting.

how to strum the ukulele

To strum, make a loose fist with your index finger extended. Brush the fingernail of your index finger across the strings towards the floor. In the examples and songs that follow you will strum four times for each chord letter that you see.

A strum mark looks like this ╱.

╱   ╱   ╱   ╱ = 4 strums

It is typical to strum over the fretboard, not the body of the ukulele.

O = leave strings open/no fingers

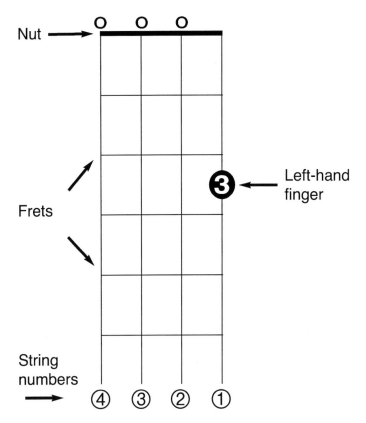

Nut →

Left-hand finger

Frets

String numbers →
④ ③ ② ①

/ = one beat strum

Strum down towards the floor from string 4 though string 1.

Track 2

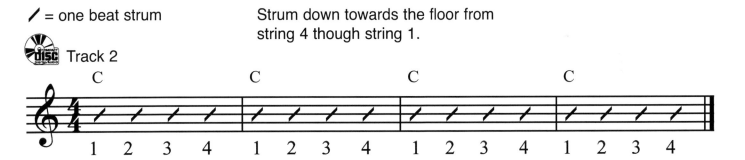

𝄽 = one beat rest

Do not strum rests.

Track 3

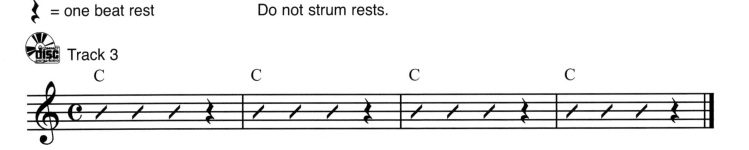

Try to make sure each chord sounds clean and clear. Make sure you are strumming through all the strings and that every string is sounding.

three blind mice

Track 4

One beat strum

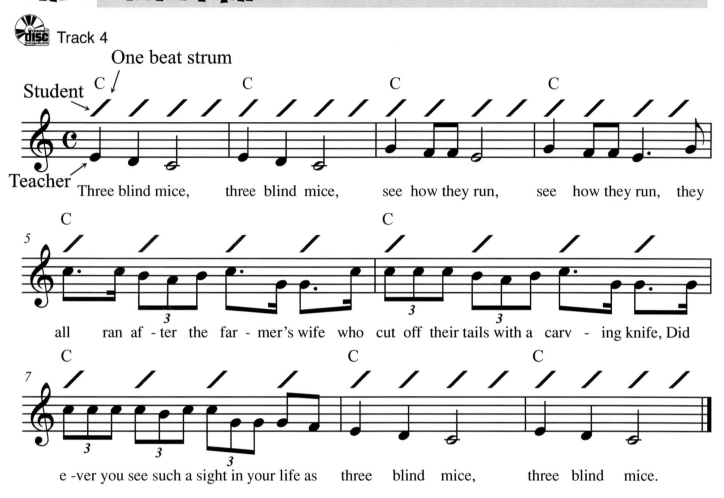

Half note rest

The half note rest looks like this ▬ . It gets two beats of rest. So ▬ = 𝄽 𝄽 (two beats).

Strum twice then rest for two beats

Track 5, Half rests

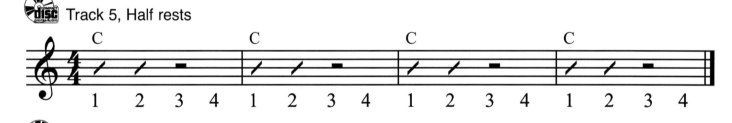

Track 6, More half rests

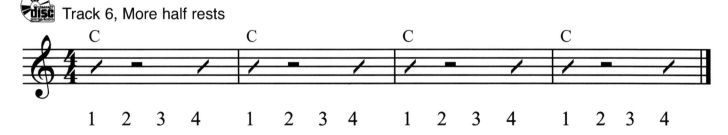

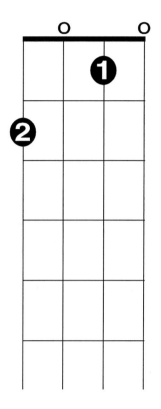

 Track 7

Whole note rest

The whole note rest looks like this ▬. (It looks like an upside down half note rest.) The whole note rest gets four beats of rest.

▬ = 𝄽 𝄽 𝄽 𝄽

 Track 8, Whole rests

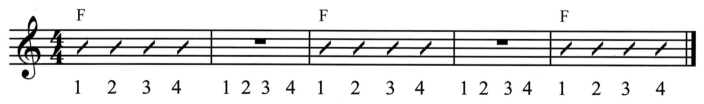

brother john (frere jacques)

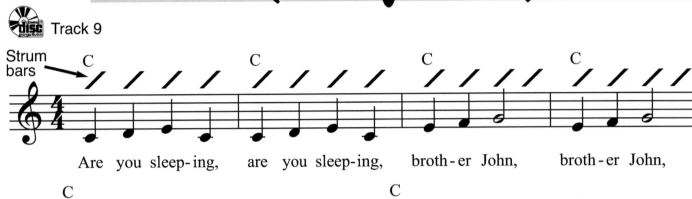

Are you sleep-ing,   are you sleep-ing,   broth-er John,   broth-er John,

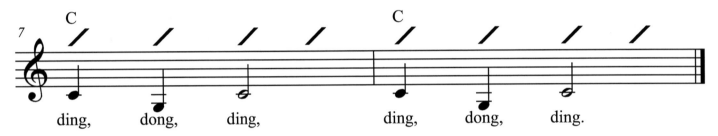

Morn-ing bells are ring - ing,   morn-ing bells are ring - ing,

ding,   dong,   ding,   ding,   dong,   ding.

Mixing Chords #1

Mixing Chords #2

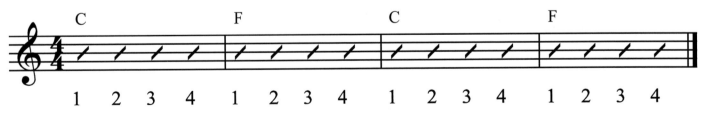

what is a measure?

A measure keeps a certain number of notes grouped together.

Time Signature: The top number tells us how many beats are in each measure.

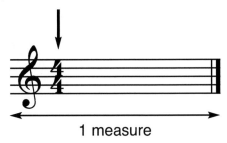

1 measure

The three most common time signatures are:

4/4 Four beats per measure

3/4 Three beats per measure

2/4 Two beats per measure

row, row, row your boat

 Track 12

This means only two strums per measure.

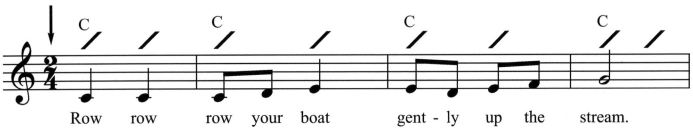

Row row row your boat gent - ly up the stream.

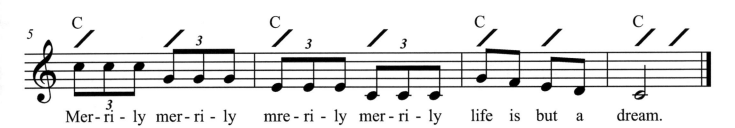

Mer - ri - ly mer - ri - ly mre - ri - ly mer - ri - ly life is but a dream.

G7 chord

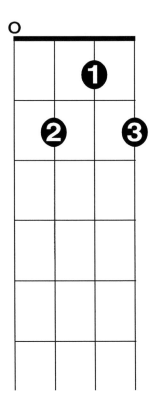

When we see strum bars in a measure they will now have stems. They still get one beat.

Track 13

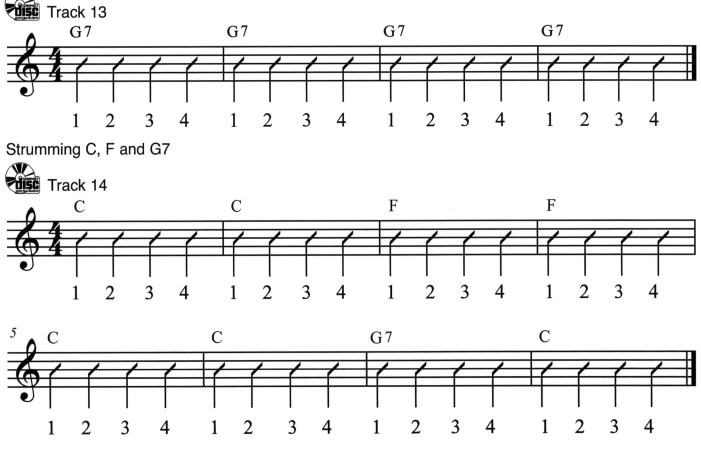

We will be using the C, F and G7 chords quite a bit. Make sure you feel comfortable with them.

pay me my money down

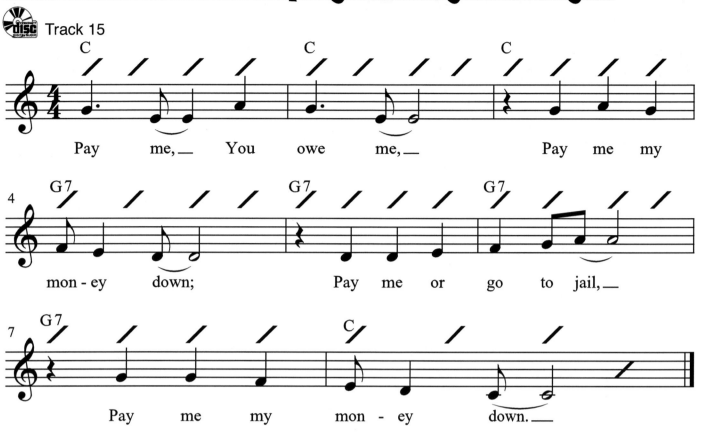

Pay me,__ You owe me,__ Pay me my mon-ey down; Pay me or go to jail,__ Pay me my mon-ey down.__

london bridge

Two strums per measure.

Lon-don bridge is fall-ing down, fall-ing down, fall-ing down, Lon-don bridge is fall-ing down. My fair la-dy.

three-chord progression

Track 17

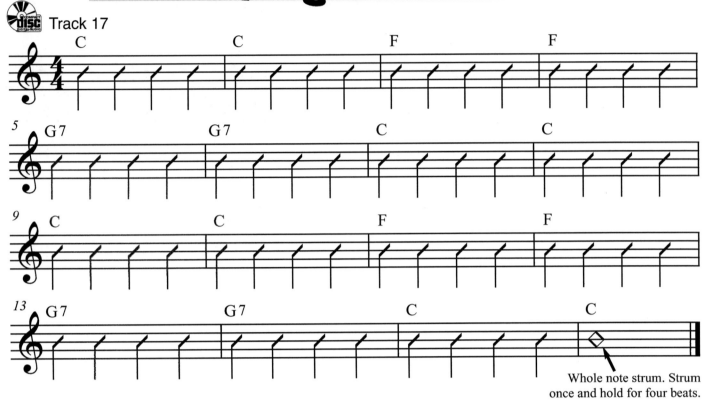

Whole note strum. Strum once and hold for four beats.

skip to my lou

Track 18

Strum four beats per measure.

Lost my part-ner, wha-t'll I do? lost my part-ner wha-t'll I do?

Lost my part-ner wha-t'll I do? skip to my Lou, my dar-ling!

Gone a-gain, skip to my Lou, Gone a-gain, skip to my Lou,

Gone a-gain, skip to my Lou, Skip to my Lou, my dar-ling!

jingle bells

 Track 19

Strum four beats per measure.

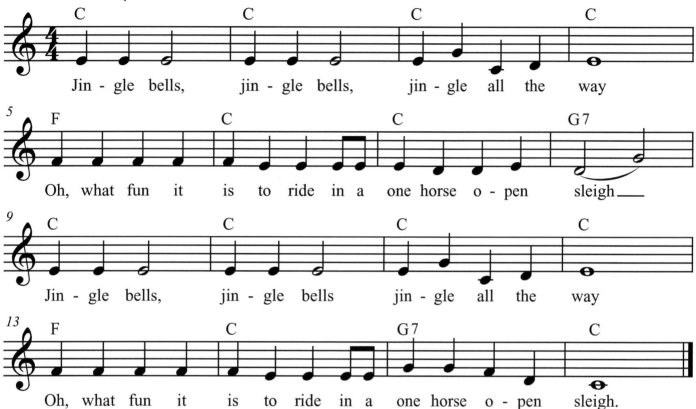

Jin - gle bells, jin - gle bells, jin - gle all the way

Oh, what fun it is to ride in a one horse o - pen sleigh___

Jin - gle bells, jin - gle bells jin - gle all the way

Oh, what fun it is to ride in a one horse o - pen sleigh.

this old man

 Track 20

Strum two beats per measure.

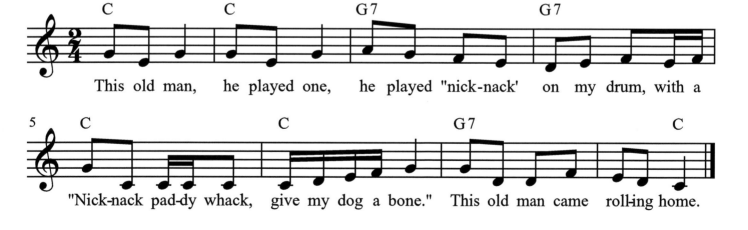

This old man, he played one, he played "nick-nack' on my drum, with a

"Nick-nack pad-dy whack, give my dog a bone." This old man came roll-ing home.

playing single notes - C

When we play single notes we are usually playing the melody which is typically the words of the song.

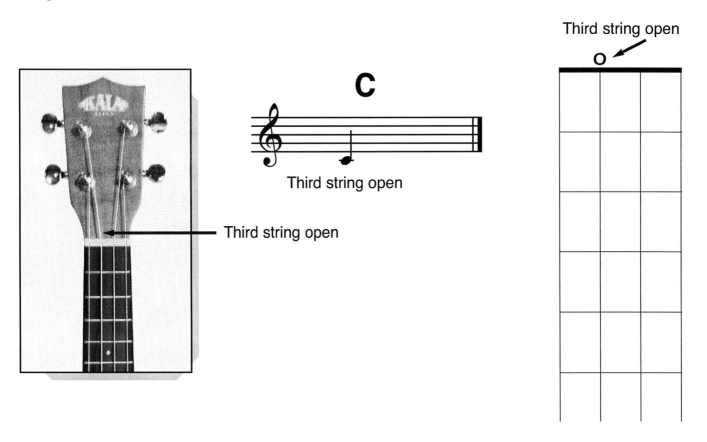

Third string open

C

Third string open

Third string open

Third string open

When playing single notes use your <u>thumb</u> to strike the string on a downward motion towards the floor.

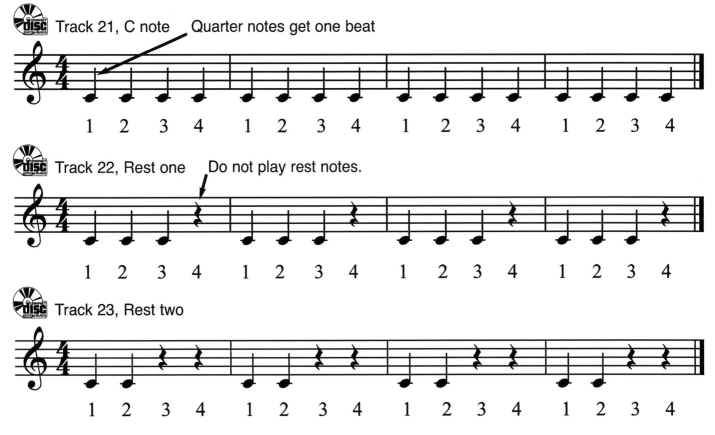

Track 21, C note   Quarter notes get one beat

1 2 3 4   1 2 3 4   1 2 3 4   1 2 3 4

Track 22, Rest one   Do not play rest notes.

1 2 3 4   1 2 3 4   1 2 3 4   1 2 3 4

Track 23, Rest two

1 2 3 4   1 2 3 4   1 2 3 4   1 2 3 4

playing single notes - D

When playing notes and chords sometimes we will see the following symbols ⊓ and V.
⊓ = Pick or strum down.
V = Pick or strum up. We will work on this one later.

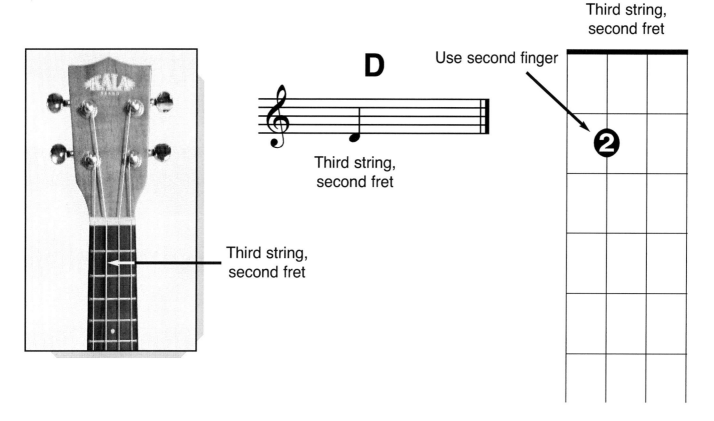

A whole note looks like this **o** it gets four beats. Pick once and let ring for four beats.

Track 24

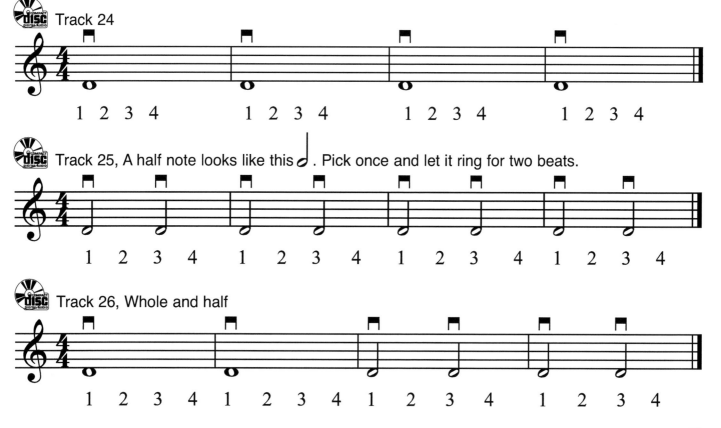

Track 25, A half note looks like this ♩. Pick once and let it ring for two beats.

Track 26, Whole and half

Track 27, C and D whole notes

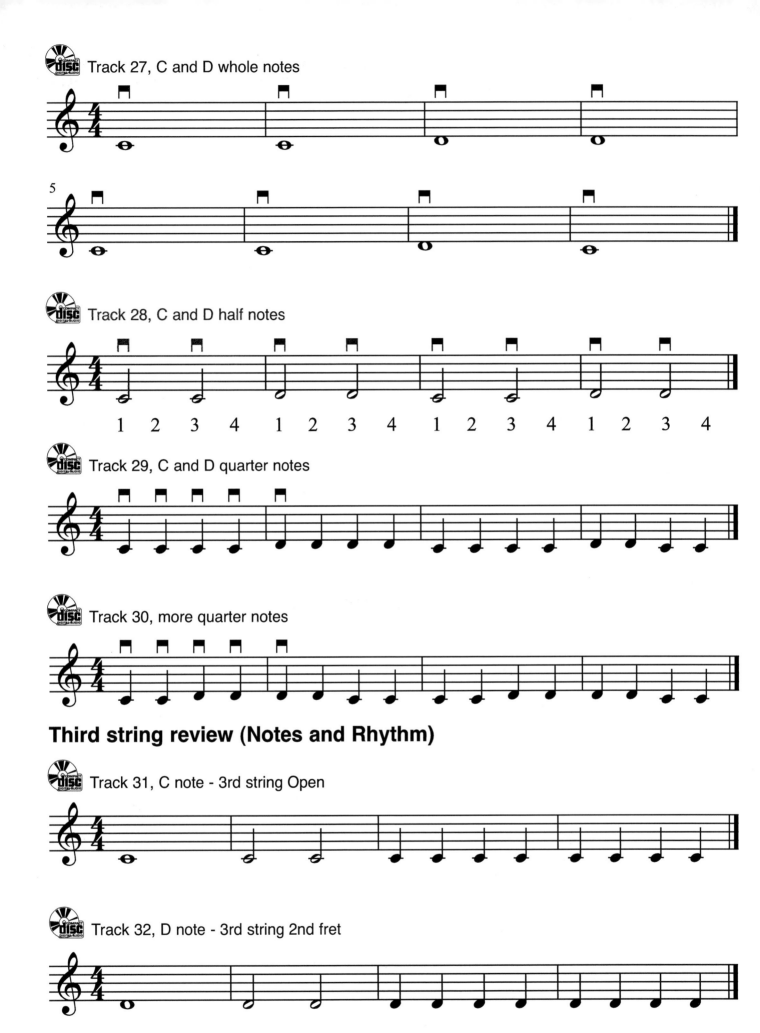

Track 28, C and D half notes

Track 29, C and D quarter notes

Track 30, more quarter notes

Third string review (Notes and Rhythm)

Track 31, C note - 3rd string Open

Track 32, D note - 3rd string 2nd fret

3/4 time

So far we have played songs mostly in 4/4 time, meaning four beats to a measure. Let's play some tunes in 3/4.

$\frac{3}{4}$ = 3 beats to a measure.

it's raining, it's pouring

 Track 33

This is a pickup measure. It is not a full measure, it is missing some beats. Begin strumming after the pickup note is played. Strum three beats per measure.

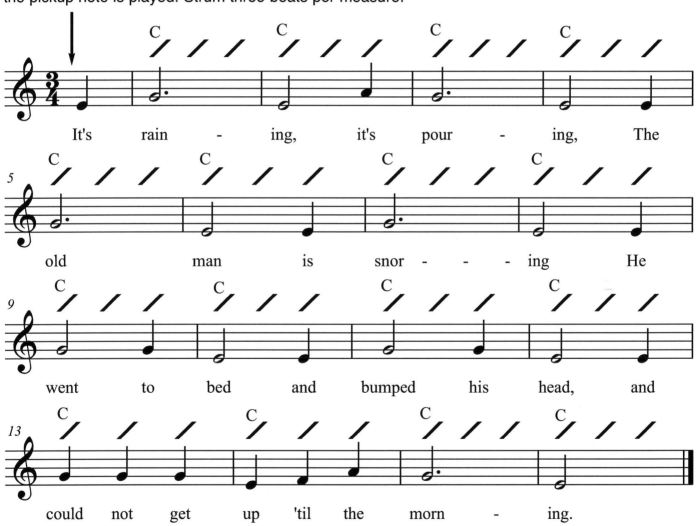

G chord

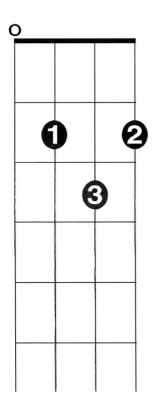

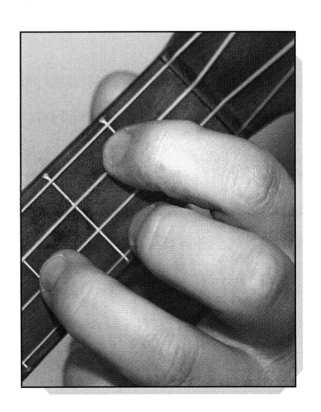

The G chord is a triangle shape similar to the shape of the G7 chord.

Track 34

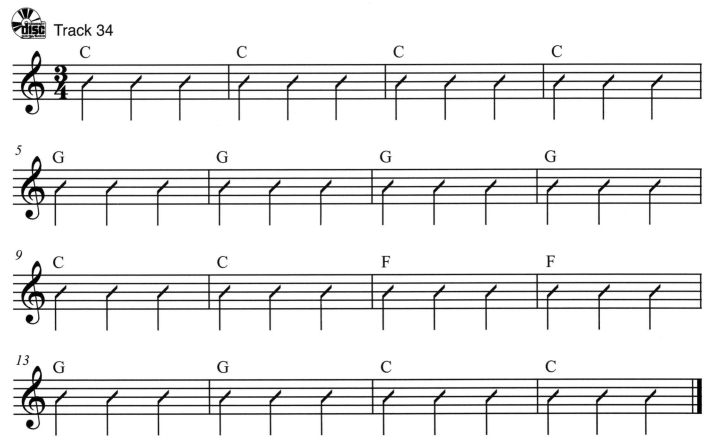

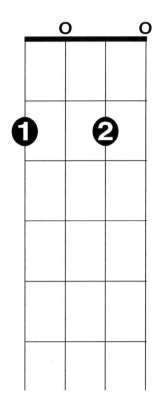

ten little ukuleles

 Track 35

Strum four beats per measure.

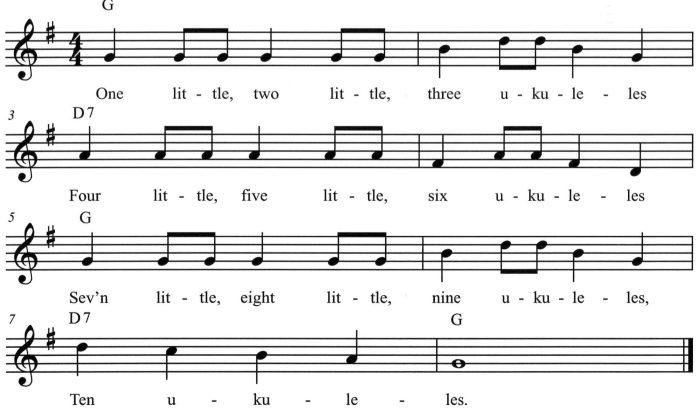

One lit - tle, two lit - tle, three u - ku - le - les

Four lit - tle, five lit - tle, six u - ku - le - les

Sev'n lit - tle, eight lit - tle, nine u - ku - le - les,

Ten u - ku - le - les.

down in the valley

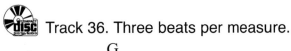 Track 36. Three beats per measure.

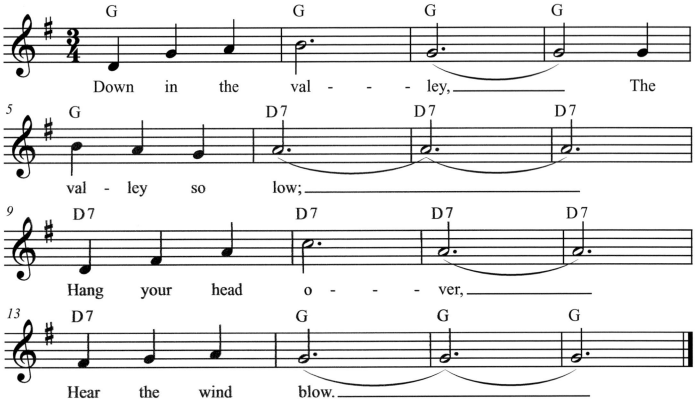

Down in the val - - ley, _____ The

val - ley so low; _____

Hang your head o - - - ver, _____

Hear the wind blow. _____

on top of old smoky

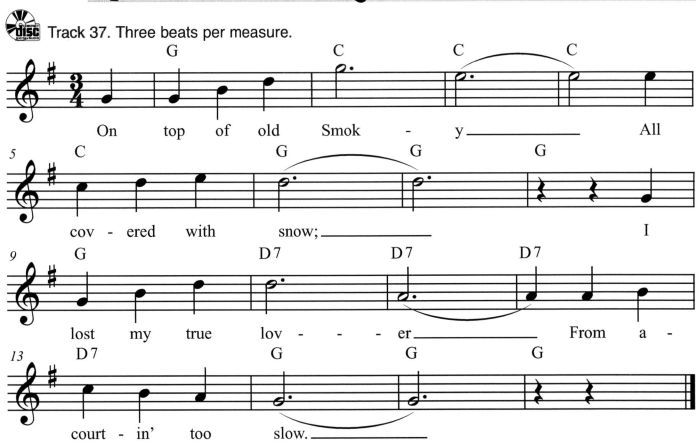 Track 37. Three beats per measure.

On top of old Smok - y _____ All

cov - ered with snow; _____ I

lost my true lov - - er _____ From a -

court - in' too slow. _____

22

playing single notes - E

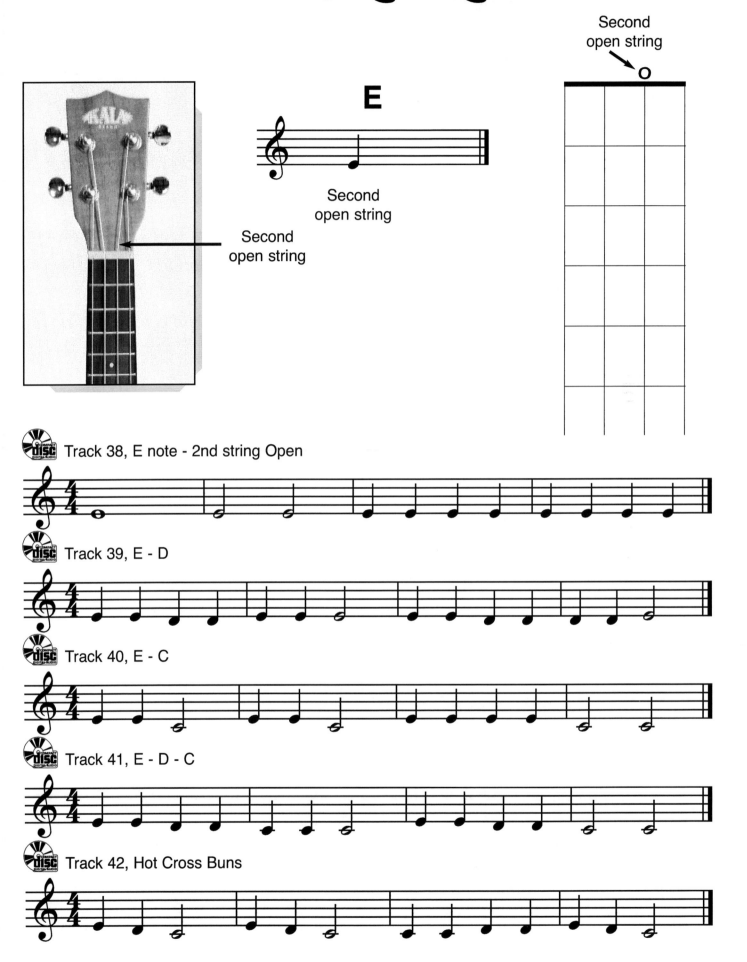

playing single notes - F

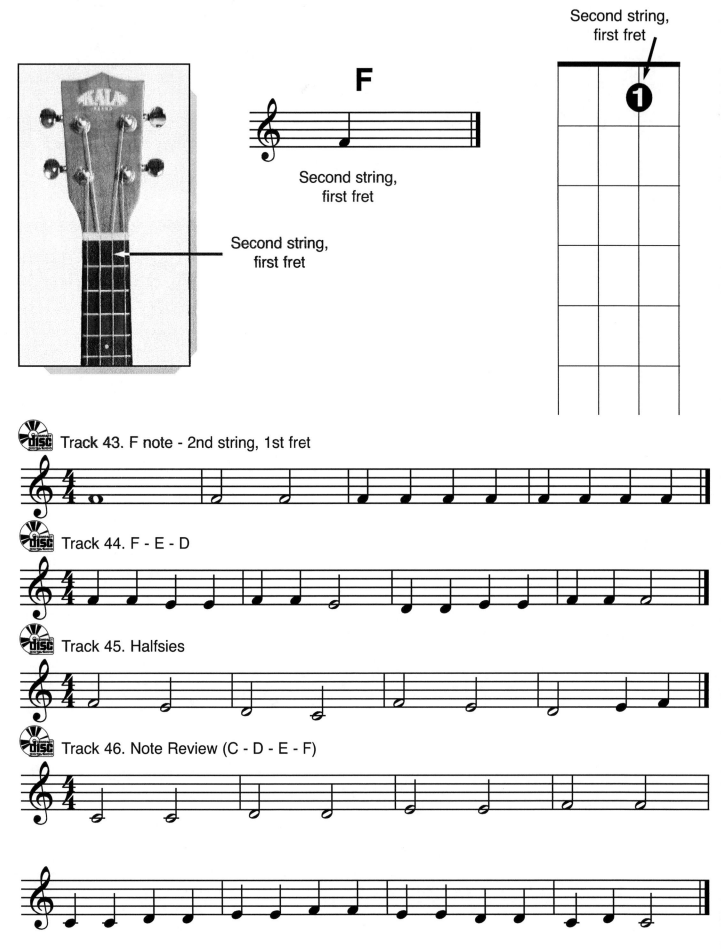

F

Second string,
first fret

Second string,
first fret

Second string,
first fret

Track 43. F note - 2nd string, 1st fret

Track 44. F - E - D

Track 45. Halfsies

Track 46. Note Review (C - D - E - F)

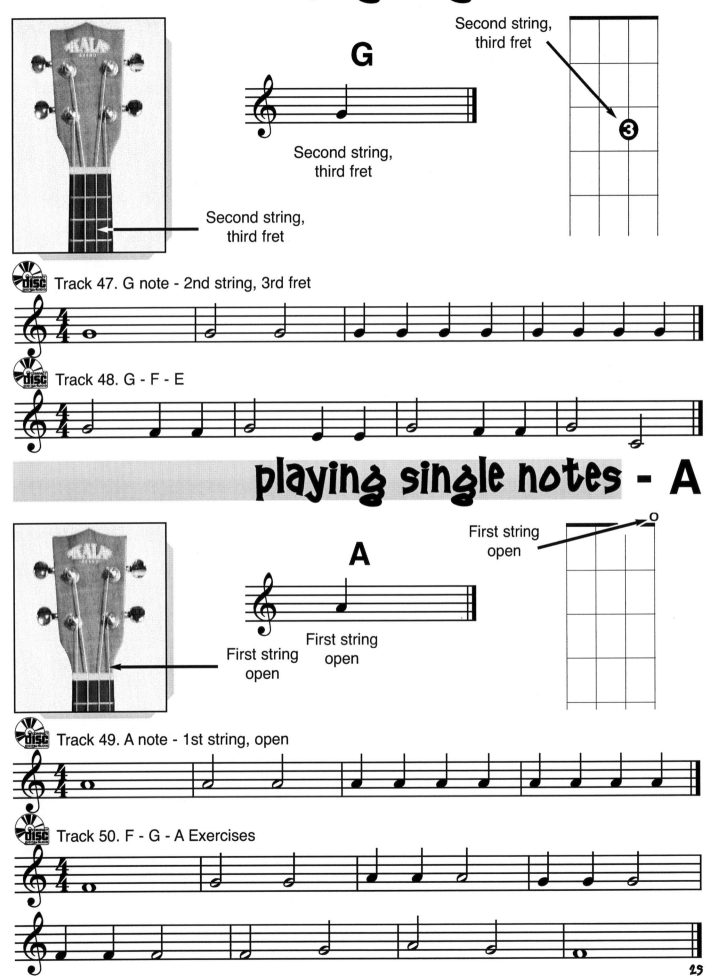

G

Second string, third fret

Second string, third fret

Second string, third fret

Track 47. G note - 2nd string, 3rd fret

Track 48. G - F - E

A

First string open

First string open

First string open

Track 49. A note - 1st string, open

Track 50. F - G - A Exercises

twinkle, twinkle little star

jingle bells

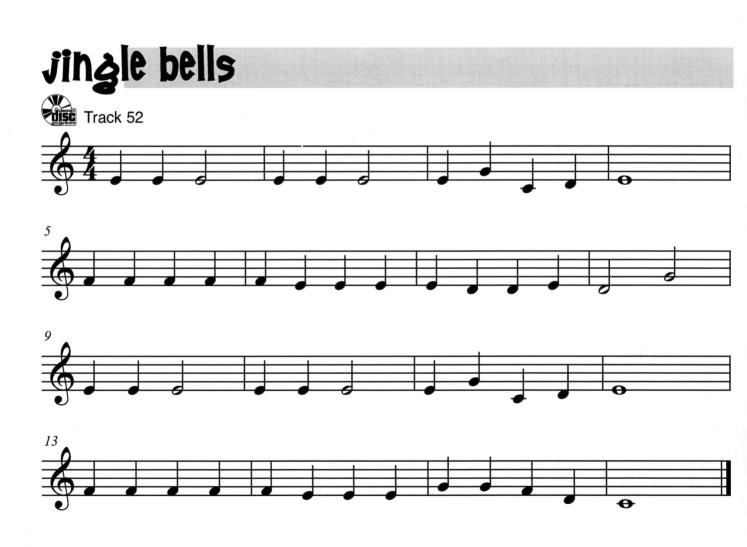

There are many ways to strum chords using different strum patterns. We know one pattern for strumming in 4/4 it is:

Strum Pattern #1

Let's learn a new strum pattern.
Strum Pattern #2

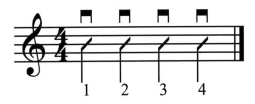

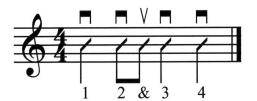

Reminder: ⊓ = strum up
　　　　　 V = strum down

We have added tails to our strum slashes. This helps us with our new rhythms. Now they look more like notes, but still have slashes.

Up Strums

When strumming up use the fingertip/pad of your index finger. Bring your finger across the strings toward the ceiling. It is not necessary to hit all four strings, you only need to strum the first two or three strings.

Let's practice our new strum rhythm. The recorded examples will use strum pattern #2 for songs in 4/4 from now on.

Track 53

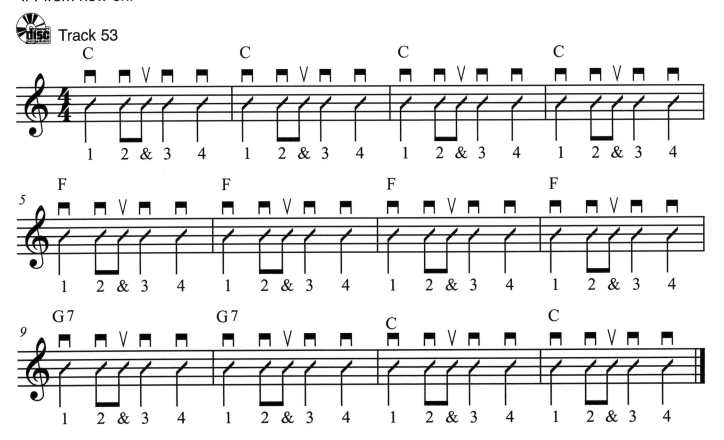

polly wolly doodle

Four beats per measure. Use strum pattern #2.

when the saints go marching in

 Track 55

Four beats per measure. Use strum pattern #2.

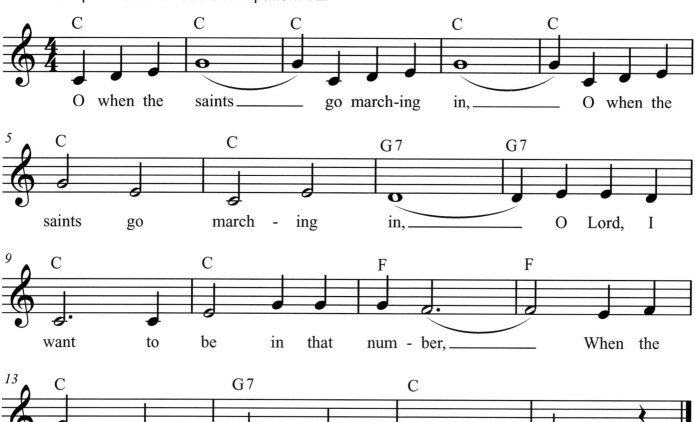

O when the saints ____ go march-ing in, ____ O when the

saints go march - ing in, ____ O Lord, I

want to be in that num - ber, ____ When the

saints go march - ing in. ____

careless love

Track 56

Strum four beats per measure.

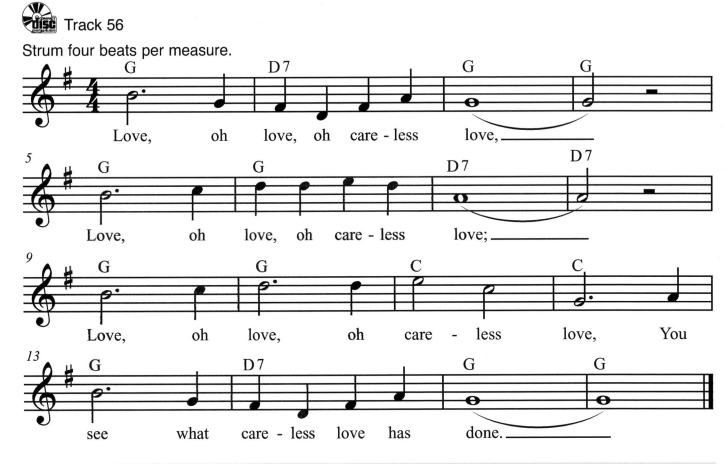

Love, oh love, oh care - less love,

Love, oh love, oh care - less love;

Love, oh love, oh care - less love, You

see what care - less love has done.

corinne, corinna

Track 57

Strum four beats per measure.

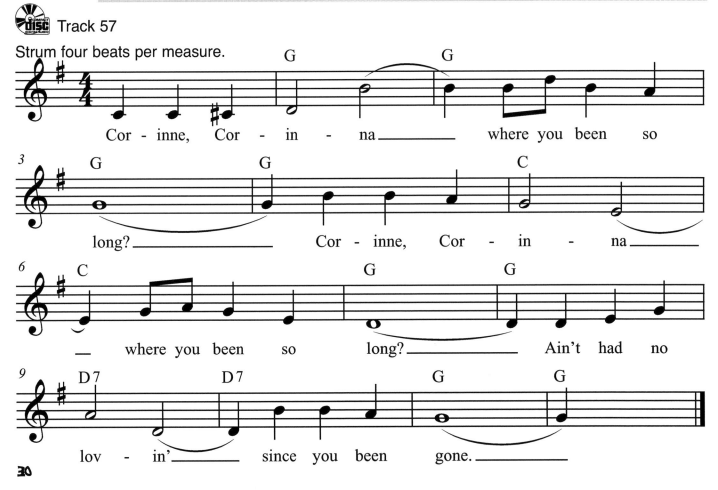

Cor - inne, Cor - in - na where you been so

long? Cor - inne, Cor - in - na

— where you been so long? Ain't had no

lov - in' since you been gone.

playing single notes - B

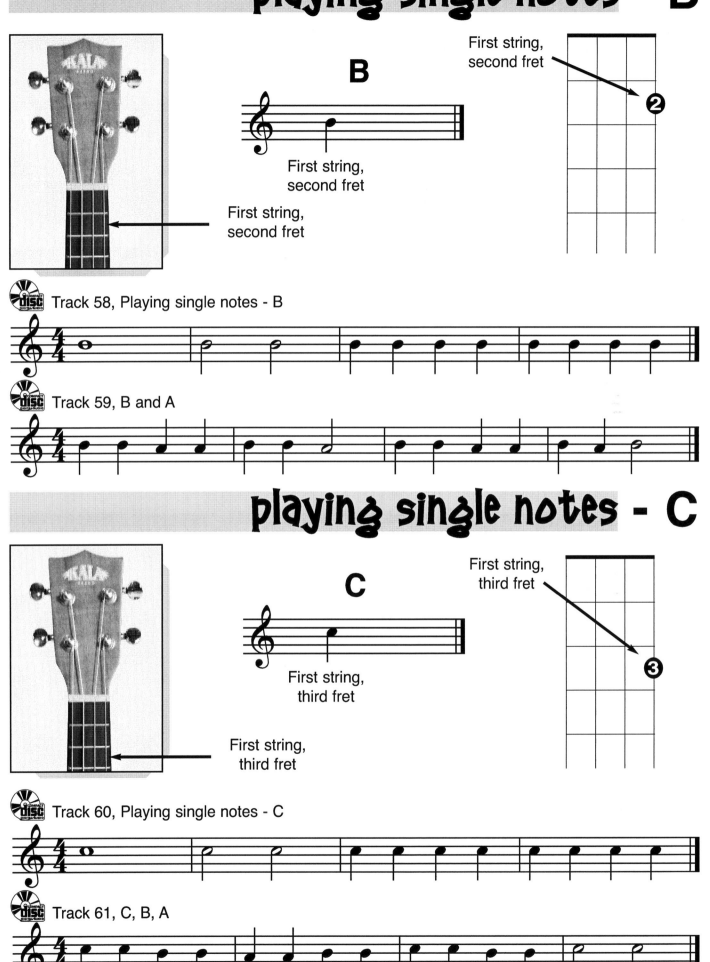

B

First string, second fret

First string, second fret

First string, second fret

Track 58, Playing single notes - B

Track 59, B and A

playing single notes - C

C

First string, third fret

First string, third fret

First string, third fret

Track 60, Playing single notes - C

Track 61, C, B, A

all the notes

the bridge melody

happy uke

new 3/4 strum pattern

Here is a new strum pattern for songs in 3/4.

Track 65

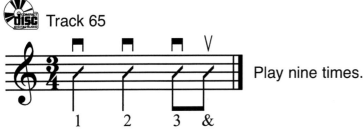

Play nine times.

home on the range

Track 66

Oh give me a home where the buf-fa-lo roam, where the deer and the an-te-lope play___ Where sel-dom is heard a dis-cour-ag-ing word and the skies are not cloud-y all day.___ Home, home on the range___ where the deer and the an-te-lope play___ where sel-dom is heard a dis-cour-ag-ing word and the skies are not cloud-y all day.___

my bonnie

Strum three beats per measure. Use the 3/4 strum pattern.

oh, my darling clementine

 Track 68

Strum three beats per measure.

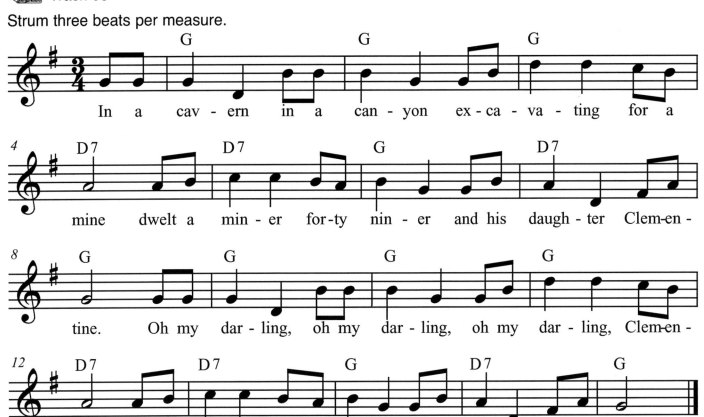

In a cav - ern in a can - yon ex - ca - va - ting for a
mine dwelt a min - er for-ty nin - er and his daugh - ter Clem-en -
tine. Oh my dar - ling, oh my dar - ling, oh my dar - ling, Clem-en -
tine, you are lost and gone for - ev - er oh my dar-ling Clem-en - tine.

about the author

Lee "Drew" Andrews is a multi-instrumentalist with a day job. He is head editor at Mel Bay Publications, where he has been for the last 7 years. He has written over twenty best-selling books for ukulele, guitar, mandolin, banjo, Dobro® and more. At the 2009 Winter NAMM show three of his Children's Chord books, one being ukulele, won a Best in Show award. Drew plays with the Polynesian revue "A Touch of Paradise". He plays ukulele, bass and percussion. With this group he has played for US Senators and Congressmen as well as foreign heads of state. Most recently they played at the International Steel Guitar Convention in St. Louis, Missouri backing up the world-famous Hawaiian steel player L.T. Zinn. Drew is also an in-demand teacher. Be sure to visit the author's website www.UkuleleVillage.com.

Photo credit: Gary W. Davis